A Painful History of Medicine

Scalpels, Stitches & Scars

a history of surgery

EXPRESS EDITION

John Townsend

Raintree

Chicago, Illinois

Printed and bound in China by South China
Printing Company

10 09 08 07 06
10 9 8 7 6 5 4 3 2 1

The Library of Congress has cataloged-the
original version as follows:
Townsend, John, 1955-
 Hospitals: scalpels, stitches & scars / John
Townsend.
    p. cm -- (A painful history of medicine)
 Includes bibliographical references and index.
 ISBN 1-4109-1332-5 (library bdg.-hardcover) --
ISBN 1-4109-1337-6 (pbk.)
 1. Surgery--History--Juvenile literature.
I. Title. II Series:
Townsend, John, 1955-
Painful History of Medicine
 RD21.T69 2005
 617'09--dc22
 2004014248

10-digit ISBN 1 410 92542 0 (hardback)
13-digit ISBN 978 1 4109 2542 8

10-digit ISBN 1 410 92547 1 (paperback)
13-digit ISBN 978 1 4109 2547 3

This leveled text is a version of *Freestyle: A Painful
History of Medicine: Scalpels, Stitches and Scars*

Acknowledgments

Alamy Images/ Yoav Levy/ Phototake Inc. p. **43**;
Ancient Art and Architecture Collection
pp. **14–15**; Art Archive/ Marc Charmet p. **20**; Art
Directors and Trip pp. **18**, **23**, **38**; Bridgeman Art
Library pp. **4–5** (Giraudon), **18–19** (Musee de
L'Hotel Sandelin); Corbis pp. **24–25**, **26–27**, **31**
(Bettman), **32**, **33** (Michael Crabtree), **34–35**
(Medford Historical Society Collection), **40–41**
(Bettman), **42** (Michael Crabtree), **45** (Rufus
F. Folkks), **50** (Reuters), **51** (ER Productions), **53**
(Michael Crabtree); Hulton Archive pp. **12**, **19**,
28, **36–37**, **37**; Mary Evans Picture Library pp. **6**,
25; Medical on Line pp. **9**, **10**, **11**, **21**, **32–33**,
44–45, **46–47**; Medizip Surgerical Zipper p. **48**;
Reuters/ Chris Helgren p. **16**; Science Photo
Library pp. **6–7** (National Museum, Denmark/
Munoz-Yague), **8–9** (Dr Morley Read), **13** (Jerry
Mason), **16–17**, **22**, **29** (CNRI), **30** (AJ Photo),
36 (Stanley B Burns, MD & The Burns Archive
New York), **41** (Custom Medical Stock Photo),
42–43 (BSIP, Laurent), **47** (David M Martin,
MD), **48–49** (Pascal Goetgheluck), **49** (H Raguet/
Eurelios); The Kobal Collection pp. **10–11**
(Dreamworks/ Universal/ Buitendijk, Jaap), **15**
(Warner Bros.); The Queen Victoria Hospital p.
38–39; Wellcome Library, London pp. **8**, **12–13**,
24, **26**, **28–29**.

Cover photograph of Guinea Pig Club patients
reproduced with permission of The Queen
Victoria Hospital Museum.

Every effort has been made to contact copyright
holders of any material reproduced in this book.
Any omissions will be rectified in subsequent
printings if notice is given to the publishers.

The paper used to print this book comes from
sustainable resources.

Disclaimer

All the Internet addresses (URLs) given in this
book were valid at the time of going to press.
However, due to the dynamic nature of the
Internet, some addresses may have changed, or
sites may have changed or ceased to exist since
publication. While the author and publishers
regret any inconvenience this may cause readers,
no responsibility for any such changes can be
accepted by either the author or the publishers.

Contents

Any words appearing in the text in bold, **like this**, are explained in the glossary. You can also look out for them in the Word bank at the bottom of each page.

Cutting Open

The scalpel

Surgeons use a small knife to cut bodies open. It is called a scalpel. Today scalpels are made from steel. Thousands of years ago, they were made from bone or flint (a type of hard rock).

Our bodies are a bit like cars when they go wrong. A **surgeon** may need to look inside. A surgeon is a doctor who operates on the body. Parts of the body may have to be patched up. They may need to be taken away and replaced.

Surgery makes us think of **scalpels**, blood, and needles. Surgery today is far safer than it was in the past.

This drawing from 1368 shows an operation taking place.

Blood and guts

In the past surgery was very risky. You were awake during an operation. Strong men held you down while the blade cut into you. You screamed in agony.

Surgeons never washed their hands before they operated. They had to stitch you up quickly. Otherwise you would bleed to death.

find out later...

...why surgeons had to cut legs off so fast.

...why barbers tried to make customers bleed.

...why surgeons don't always use scalpels today.

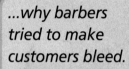

scalpel   knife with a small, sharp blade

Thousands of years ago people tried to treat pain. But they had to guess how to do it. Some people learned how to do very basic surgery. They only found out what worked best by trying it out. Today **surgeons** are very skilful. This is because of hundreds of years of blood and pain.

Skulls

Ancient skulls with holes cut in them have been found all over the world. In some the bone had started to grow back around the holes. This shows that these patients **survived**.

Drilling a hole through a patient's skull in 1880.

Holes in the head

Skulls have been found with holes drilled in them. They are from people who died 10,000 years ago. Some of these skulls have up to five holes.

Why did people drill holes in peoples' heads? They may have done it to let out "evil spirits." They might have done it to cure bad headaches. The name of this operation is **trepanning**.

This skull was trepanned over 1,000 years ago.

Easing the pressure

In 1998 Hayden McGlinn was playing football. He hit his head and collapsed. A doctor thought Hayden was bleeding inside his brain. He drilled a hole into Hayden's head to let out the **pressure**. This did the trick!

pressure force that builds up in a space and cannot escape

7

Making use of nature

People long ago did not know how to make tools for surgery. For **scalpels** they used sticks, stones, and bones.

South American Indians used army ants to hold wounds together. The ants were held over two flaps of skin. When they bit, their jaws clamped the wound shut. The Indians pinched off the ants' bodies. The head was left behind, like a stitch in the skin.

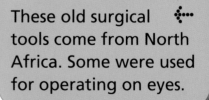

These old surgical tools come from North Africa. Some were used for operating on eyes.

Bones

If you break your arm, a doctor sets it in solid plaster. This helps the bone to mend.

But what did people do about broken arms long ago? **Aboriginal Australians** dug wet clay out of the ground. They wrapped it around the broken arm. The clay dried in the sun and set solid. It was just like a modern plaster cast.

Healing

- Egyptians used to put tree bark on wounds. This stopped them from getting **infected**.

- Aboriginal Australians put clay or animal fat over cuts. This helped the scars heal.

The army ant has strong, pincerlike jaws.

infected   when tiny living things grow in the body and cause diseases

Roman and Greek surgeons

The Greeks and Romans used surgery over 2,000 years ago. Roman **surgeons** knew how to stitch wounds. They did this to stop bleeding.

Cuts on the soldiers' arms and legs sometimes became **infected**. This happens when tiny living things get into a wound and cause diseases. Roman surgeons used knives and saws to cut off infected arms and legs.

Stitch-up

Surgeons use stitches to close up wounds (see below). Today stitches are usually made of nylon (a strong, man-made fiber). They can be used inside the body. They can also hold the skin together.

Word bank

catgut   strong thread made from the intestines of sheep. It is used in surgery.

Gladiators

Galen was a Greek surgeon. He was born about 1,900 years ago. Galen used **catgut** for stitches. He was one of the first surgeons to do this.

Galen worked for the Romans. He saved many **gladiators'** lives. Gladiators are men whom the Romans trained to fight with weapons. They often got badly injured.

Closing a wound using staples.

Did you know?

- Metal staples are quick to use. They cause fewer infections than stitches. But they can leave more scars.

- Surgical glue is the newest way to close wounds.

The Romans paid gladiators to fight. The Roman crowds liked to watch them.

gladiator   person trained to fight with weapons

The **Middle Ages** was a period in European history. It was between 500 and 1,500 years ago. There were many new ideas about medicine at this time. These ideas came from Arab **surgeons**. Arabs were people from the Middle East.

Arab surgeons set bones and stitched wounds. They did many other things, too. They even operated on eyes.

Ouch!

Arab surgeons pressed red-hot irons into wounds (see picture above). They did this to seal them up. It was supposed to stop wounds becoming **infected** with **bacteria**.

Word bank

infected when tiny living things grow in the body and cause diseases

Learning surgery

The Arab surgeons wrote down their new treatments. European monks made copies of these books. The books became important for training doctors.

By AD 1300 surgeons had learned a lot about the body. They did not learn only from books. Some doctors cut up dead bodies. Then they could see what went on inside.

Hit and miss

Arab doctors were not keen to cut people open. They knew the shock and bleeding could kill. If they did operate, they drugged the patient with **opium**. This is a drug made from poppies (below).

These surgeons ⋯ are cutting a boil on a man's head.

bacteria group of tiny living things that can cause diseases

Chop it off

There were many battles in the **Middle Ages**. **Surgeons** treated the wounds of soldiers on battlefields. Arrows caused many wounds. Taking out arrowheads caused a lot of damage to the body.

Wounds often became **infected**. Surgeons had to chop off infected parts of the body to save lives. This is called **amputation**.

On the move

From the 10th century onward, surgeons started to travel around Europe. They set broken bones and pulled out teeth. People paid them for doing this.

The Arabs and Europeans fought each other 800 years ago. These battles were called the Crusades.

Word bank   **Middle Ages** period in history between about AD 500 and 1500

Sweet dreams

Amputation was very painful. Patients lost a lot of blood. They often died. Some surgeons tried to make their patients sleepy before an amputation. They used mixtures of herbs, drugs, and wine. Often these just allowed the patient to die more peacefully.

Saddle-sore

In the Middle Ages, people traveled a long way on horses (see below). This sometimes caused infections in their **rectums**. One surgeon treated patients by cutting a hole between the rectum and buttock. This made going to the toilet easier.

rectum end part of the large intestine. It is joined to the anus.

Gunshot wounds

People started to use handguns in the 1300s. This caused **surgeons** a lot of problems. They had to learn how to treat gunshot wounds.

Surgeons had to dig out bullets. This caused the wounds to get **infected**. Then **gangrene** would set in. This is when the flesh rots and dies. To stop the gangrene, surgeons cut off infected arms or legs.

Not everyone died when they got shot. But many died when their gunshot wounds became infected.

Word bank   blood vessel   narrow tube inside the body that carries blood

Burning oil

Many doctors poured boiling oil into wounds. This was to seal them. Then they would not bleed or get gangrene. It worked, but patients got bad burns.

Ambroise Paré was a surgeon in the 1500s. He stopped using hot oil to seal wounds. He thought it caused too much damage. Instead, Paré tied up the **blood vessels** quickly.

A better way

Ambroise Paré ran out of hot oil one day. Instead, he made a mixture. It was made of egg yolk, oil of roses, and **turpentine**. Paré put this onto his patients' wounds. He found it was better than hot oil. It caused less pain. Also his patients' wounds did not become sore and swollen.

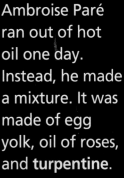

If blood cannot reach a part of the body, gangrene can set in.

turpentine oil and resin mixture that comes from pine trees

From the 1500s to the 1700s, barbers cut more than just hair. They also cut out boils and made cuts in the skin. They were called **barber surgeons**.

People thought that too much blood made them ill. They thought bleeding was good for them. Cutting people to let blood flow out was called **bloodletting**. Barber surgeons did bloodletting.

Bloodletting

Barbers did bloodletting. They tied a strap around the arm. This made the veins swell. The fattest vein was opened with a blade. Then the blood spurted out.

Bruegel painted this picture in 1556. It is making fun of barber surgeons.

Word bank

barber surgeon barber who also did minor surgery, mainly for the poor

Barber surgery

When a barber surgeon did an operation, his bandages got covered in blood. He would hang them from a post to dry. The wind twirled the bandages around the post. They made a red and white spiral pattern.

Later this pattern was painted on poles. These showed where a barber worked. Some barbers today still have red and white poles outside their shops.

Being bled

Samuel Pepys (above) wrote about London life in the 1600s. Samuel was bled by a barber. He wrote about it in his diary.

4 May 1662

Mr Holliard came to let me bleed. I began to be sick, but lying on my back, I was soon well again. I gave him 5 shillings and he left.

bloodletting   cutting the skin or a vein to let blood flow out

All in a day's work

In the 1600s London had only two main hospitals. They did not have any special rooms for operating. Most surgery was done at home or in barber shops.

Joseph Binns was a **surgeon**. He worked from 1633 to 1663. In one notebook he made a list of his patients' problems.

77 patients with swellings
15 with battle wounds
14 injured at work
41 hurt in fights
19 fallen from horses

Hot treatment

People used to think burning wounds was a good idea. They used hot irons to do this. Sometimes it did seal up **blood vessels**. This stopped heavy bleeding. But often it just hurt!

This picture was drawn in 1660. It shows a surgeon sealing a wound with a red-hot iron.

Word bank

pus thick green or yellow liquid made by infected wounds. It often smells foul.

Red-hot poker

Binns treated most of his patients in his house. People got boils. Boils are painful lumps on the skin. They are caused by **bacteria**. Having a boil **lanced** was painful. Binns dug his **scalpel** into the swelling. Then he drained out the **pus**.

Binns might have poked the boil with a red-hot poker. The heat of the poker would have helped kill any germs. This helped **sterilize**, or clean, the wound. But the pain would have been terrible.

Burning flesh

Doctors still burn patients today. They use a chemical. They also use hot electric wires, or **lasers**. This is called **cauterizing**. It is only used for minor problems like warts.

Surgeons still burn away some skin problems.

laser   very strong beam of light that is used in surgery for burning or cutting

Under the knife

Sometimes a lump grows in the kidney. This is a kidney stone. It is painful if it starts to move. Samuel Pepys had a kidney stone in 1658. He needed an operation to remove it.

An operation at that time was very dangerous. There were no drugs to stop the pain. Samuel was lucky. He **survived** the surgery.

The kidneys

The two kidneys are in the lower back. They are on either side of the spine. The kidneys take out waste from the body. They keep our blood clean.

This X-ray shows the two kidneys. The orange lump in the left kidney is a large kidney stone.

Kidneys on the table

Samuel Pepys wanted to see what kidneys looked like. In 1663 he went to watch a **surgeon** cut open a dead body. He wrote about this visit in his diary:

I touched the dead body with my bare hand. It felt cold and unpleasant. Then the kidneys were placed on the table. There the surgeon showed me the kidney stone and the cutting he did to remove it.

A kidney stone is a hard lump of **calcium crystals**.

Kidney stones

Stones growing in the kidney can block it. Then the kidney might swell up or be damaged.

Patients used to need an operation to remove a kidney stone. Now stones are usually removed using very high sound waves. These are called **ultrasounds**. They break up the stones.

calcium crystals material that also makes up bones and teeth

Today patients have a good chance of getting through surgery. But it took a long time for **surgeons** to learn the best way of doing things.

Shortage of bodies

The training of surgeons got better in the 1700s. **Medical** students cut open dead bodies. They did this to see how they worked. At that time it was hard to find fresh bodies to use.

Doctor Knox bought many bodies. He used them to teach student doctors.

Word bank   **medical**   about the treatment of diseases and injuries

Body snatchers

Robert Knox was a surgeon in Scotland. In the 1820s students paid to go to his talks. During his talks he cut open bodies to show all the **organs**.

Knox bought the bodies from two thieves named Burke and Hare. At first Burke and Hare stole these bodies from graves. Then they started to kill people. The police arrested Burke and Hare in 1828.

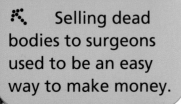

Selling dead bodies to surgeons used to be an easy way to make money.

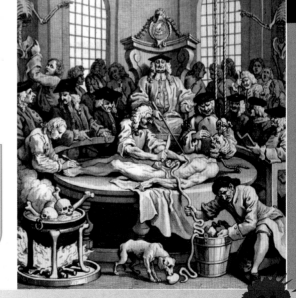

anatomy study of the structure of an animal or plant

Dull the pain

Pain and shock used to kill many patients during operations. It was not possible to do major surgery.

Horace Wells was a dentist in the United States. In 1845 he used a gas to put a patient to sleep. It was called **nitrous oxide.** The next year another American dentist put his patients to sleep. He used a chemical called **ether.** This was the start of pain-free surgery.

Teaching at the Bellevue Medical Center, New York, in 1898.

Word bank   **anesthetic**   drug to make patients sleep or to make treatment less painful

Painless surgery

Putting patients to sleep was a big risk. Too much ether would kill them. If patients had too little, they might wake up during the operation.

In 1846 **surgeons** began using ether for big operations. This was the beginning of proper **anesthetics**. Anesthetics are the drugs that stop people from feeling pain during operations.

New anesthetic

In 1847 James Simpson made a big discovery. He found out that **chloroform** could put people to sleep. In 1853 Queen Victoria was given chloroform. This was when she was giving birth to her eighth child.

This patient is waiting for surgery. He is under anesthetic at the Metropolitan Hospital in London.

chloroform   colorless liquid with a strong smell, used as an anesthetic

Cut it out

Robert Liston was a **surgeon**. He worked in London in the 1840s. For a while he did operations without using **anesthetic**.

Liston was well known. He was the fastest surgeon at the time. He once removed a huge **tumor** from a patient. It weighed 44 pounds (20 kilograms). Liston took just four minutes to cut away this tumor.

Too much rush

Robert Liston (above) once cut off a leg in less than two minutes. But he also cut off the fingers of his assistant. His work was easier when he used anesthetic. Then he could take his time!

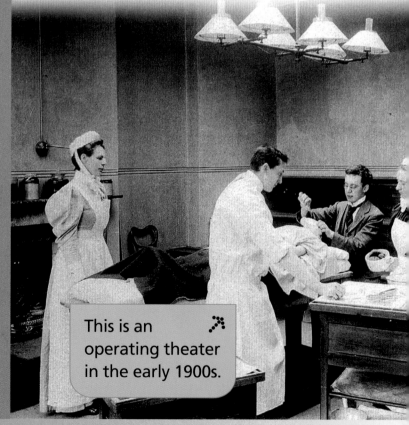

This is an operating theater in the early 1900s.

Word bank   gall bladder   organ that stores bile. This helps in digestion.

Progress

In the 1800s, surgeons began to do new operations.

- In 1882 the first **gall bladder** was removed. Carl Langenbach did the operation in Germany.

- 1n 1883 Abraham Groves took out the first **appendix**. He did this operation in Canada. The patient was a twelve-year-old boy.

Appendix

The appendix can get **infected**. This used to be very dangerous. Today surgeons can remove the appendix safely.

This is an infected appendix. It needs to be removed quickly.

appendix   organ attached to the large intestine. It has no use in the human body.

Keep it clean

Surgeons did not know about germs for a long time. They did not wash their hands. They spread harmful **bacteria** from one patient to another. These tiny living things got into wounds. Patients often died.

Thomas Spencer Wells was an English surgeon. By 1860 he washed before every operation. He saw that patients got much better if everything was clean.

Mystery

Joseph Lister was a surgeon in Scotland. He saw that many patients did not die from the operation. Instead they died from their wounds. He wanted to know why this was. He began to look for answers.

Surgeons today "scrub up" before every operation.

Word bank   **carbolic acid** chemical that can kill bacteria

Killing germs

In 1865 a cart ran over James Greenless in Scotland. It broke his leg. Wounds like this often became badly **infected**. Then the whole leg would have to be cut off.

James was lucky. A surgeon called Joseph Lister treated his leg. Lister put a special bandage on the leg. This had **carbolic acid** on it. Carbolic acid is a chemical that kills bacteria. It is called an **antiseptic**. James's wound did not get infected.

Recovery

In the 1860s Lister began to use antiseptics. He used carbolic acid in a spray. He cleaned the operating room with it (see below). As a result, more of his patients lived.

antiseptic chemical that stops harmful bacteria growing and spreading disease

Gloves and gowns

William Halsted was an American surgeon (below). In 1890 he was the first person to wear rubber gloves to operate. Surgeons also began to wear gowns and masks. This stopped doctors from spreading germs.

New ideas

Louis Pasteur was a French scientist. He found out where tiny germs or **bacteria** grew. They grew in warm, wet, dirty places. Open wounds were just like this. Bacteria bred in the wounds. Wounds became **infected**.

In 1874 Pasteur found out how to kill the germs on the tools used for surgery. He put them in boiling water. Sometimes he passed them through a flame.

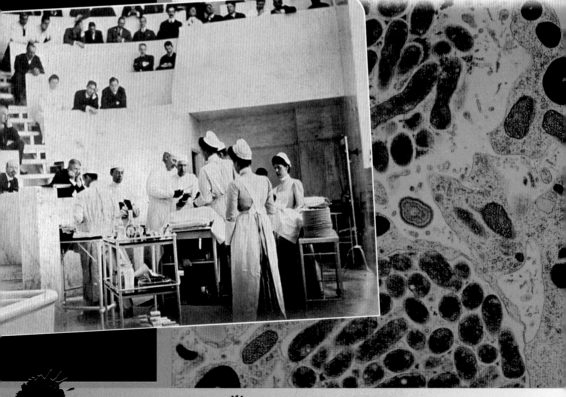

Word bank   sterilize   make clean by killing germs

Germ-free

Robert Koch was a German scientist. He found out which bacteria caused wounds to become infected. Koch also found out that hot steam was very good at killing bacteria.

Surgeons now knew it was very important to keep operating rooms clean. Bandages, tools, and clothes were all **sterilized**. Sterilizing killed bacteria and removed dirt.

Dressed to kill germs

A surgeon might cough or sneeze during an operation. This could put bacteria into a patient's open wound. Modern masks (above) have chemicals in them. These kill bacteria.

These are growing bacteria. They are seen through a microscope.

Some of the worst wounds happen
during wars. Surgery has had to get
better because of war injuries.

Wounded soldiers were taken to **field
hospitals.** These were set up close to
battles. They were often in tents.

Many soldiers got shot. The bullet
wounds soon became **infected. Surgeons**
had to deal with patients as fast
they could.

This early
photograph
shows surgeons
and patients in
the American
Civil War.

field hospital   temporary hospital, often in a
tent near the battlefield

Speed saved lives

Surgeons had to treat arms or legs that were injured. Often they cut them off. This had to be done within 24 hours of injury. Patients who waited longer were likely to die. Even then only half the patients lived. Surgeons had to find ways of working faster.

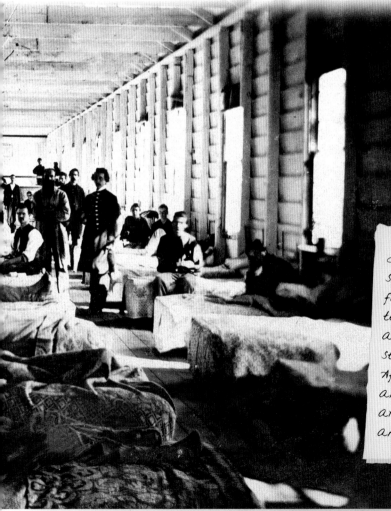

Gettysburg

There were many big battles in the American Civil War. The Battle of Gettysburg was one of them. Over 7,000 men were killed. Carl Schurz watched a surgeon at work after the battle.

The surgeon snatched his knife from between his teeth and wiped it across his blood-stained apron. After cutting off an arm, he looked around with a sigh and said, "next!"

civil war when soldiers from the same country fight each other

World War I

World War I lasted from 1914 to 1918. In this war soldiers dug ditches, called **trenches** (below). They used them for shelter from attack. Soldiers in the trenches were targets for bombs and gunfire.

Surgeons cut off more arms and legs in World War I than in any war before. At least they had **anesthetics** that sent patients to sleep. But half the patients still died.

Fast developments

In World War I, many soldiers had wounds to the head. Because of this, eye, face, ear, nose, and throat surgery quickly improved. The photograph above shows a German soldier. He stands by a wax model. It shows his injuries before surgery.

Breakthrough

Field hospitals were very dirty. Patients' wounds soon got **infected**.

One scientist thought about this problem. He saw many infected wounds. He noticed that some **bacteria** killed other bacteria. His name was Alexander Fleming. He discovered **antibiotics** in 1928. These are drugs that kill bacteria.

X-rays

X-rays let surgeons see inside the body without cutting it. They could see where the bullets were stuck inside the patient. This made it much easier to take bullets out.

The earliest X-ray machines were used in World War I.

antibiotic medicine that kills harmful bacteria

Firebombs

In World War II, many people were burned by **firebombs**. At that time people died if burns covered more than half their body. Surgeons had to quickly find new ways of treating burns.

World War II lasted from 1939 to 1945. In this war many people suffered **shrapnel** wounds. Shrapnel are small pieces of metal. They are thrown out during an explosion.

People got shrapnel in all parts of the body. Sometimes it got into the heart. For the first time, doctors began operating on the heart.

People often got stuck in bombed buildings. Then they were badly burned.

firebomb   bomb designed to start a fire

Burns

Burns were a big problem in World War II. Many pilots survived plane crashes. Often they were badly burned. There seemed to be no hope for them.

Archie McIndoe was a **surgeon**. He treated airmen with bad burns. This often meant at least 25 operations on each patient. McIndoe changed many people's lives. His patients formed a club. They called it the Guinea Pig Club.

These are members of the Guinea Pig Club.

New skin

McIndoe cut healthy skin from one part of a patient's body. Then he planted it over a burn. Sometimes the new skin died.

McIndoe tried keeping the new skin attached to the part of the body it came from (left). This kept it alive. In time the new skin began to grow on its own.

Surgery changed a lot in the late 1900s. There were many new operations.

Transplants

Christiaan Barnard was a heart **surgeon**. He set up a heart unit in South Africa. In 1967 Barnard (below) took a heart from a dead person. Then he put the heart into a 55-year-old man. This was the first heart **transplant**. Sadly, the man died after eighteen days.

New parts

Surgeons take parts from dead peoples' bodies. Then they fit them into a living person. Years ago this did not seem possible. Now transplants are made every day.

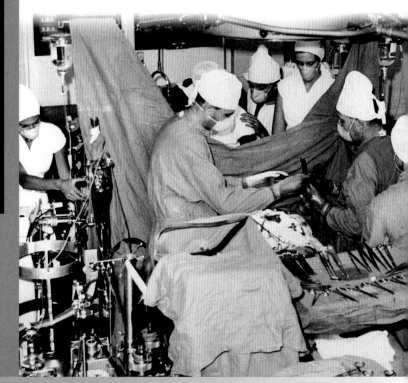

Word bank   **transplant**   when a part of a body is taken out of one person and put into another person

New hearts

Barnard tried similar operations on other patients. Many patients' bodies rejected their new hearts. This happens when the body's system for fighting infections and diseases attacks the new heart. Transplants stopped.

In 1974 a scientist in Norway found a new drug. This stopped the body from rejecting new **organs**. Heart transplants worked better. Since the 1980s most patients live for more than two years after this operation.

A dead person's organs are rushed to hospital for a transplant.

HUMAN ORGANS

organ part of the body that does a certain job

Keyhole surgery

Surgery used to make nasty wounds. It would take weeks for them to heal. They left big scars. Today **surgeons** can do operations through a very small cut. This is called keyhole surgery.

Surgeons can now see inside the body. They use a tiny camera on the end of a fine tube. It is called an **endoscope**. The surgeon watches the image on a TV screen (below).

ROCK STAR TO HAVE KEYHOLE SURGERY

Justin Hawkins is the lead singer of The Darkness. He needs surgery on his throat.

The singer canceled two shows on the band's U.S. tour. This was because of a throat problem. Surgeons will put a tiny tube into his throat. They expect him to make a full recovery.

Word bank **endoscope** instrument for seeing inside the body

Laser technology

Even the best surgeon's hand can slip. **Laser** beams can cut more accurately. A laser is a very strong beam of light. It is used in surgery for cutting or burning.

Lasers are used in many types of surgery. They have made eye surgery much safer. After a quick zap from a laser, some people no longer need to wear glasses.

Fast work

Kidney stones can now be removed easily and quickly. A tube is passed into the kidney. It takes out small stones. Larger stones need to be broken up first.

This machine breaks down large kidney stones. It uses tiny shock waves.

laser very strong beam of light that is used in surgery for cutting or burning

Plastic surgery

Plastic surgery is a type of operation. It helps to mend part of someone's body. Burns can damage skin. So can diseases or an injury. Plastic surgery can usually mend skin. **Surgeons** use **high-tech** tools to do this.

Accidents can tear off hands and fingers. Plastic surgery can help to repair them. This is called **reconstructive** surgery.

This is a diseased finger. Metal prongs are being used to straighten it.

Saving a face

In 1997 an Australian farmer caught her hair in a milking machine. It ripped off her face and her **scalp**. The scalp is the skin on top of the head. She only had her chin and one ear left. Her face and scalp were put in ice. They were rushed to hospital with her.

A top plastic surgeon successfully reattached her face and scalp. The operation took 25 hours. It was the first one of its kind.

Changing faces

People have plastic surgery for many reasons. Some want to look like film stars. In 2004 two brothers had surgery on their faces. It was to make them look like Brad Pitt.

This is the actor Brad Pitt. People have had surgery to make them look like him.

scalp skin on top of the head where the hair grows

Unblocking tubes

Our bodies are full of narrow tubes. If they clog up, they cannot work.

Some narrow tubes are called **blood vessels**. They carry our blood. Sometimes fatty lumps can block them. This puts the heart under strain.

Surgeons use a special operation to unblock blood vessels. It is called **angioplasty** (below).

Angioplasty

Surgeons use a fine tube for an angioplasty operation. It has a tiny balloon on the end. They push the tube along the blood vessel. When the tube reaches the blockage, the balloon is blown up. This pushes the blood vessel open.

During an angioplasty operation, a tiny balloon is pumped up inside a blood vessel.

Word bank   angioplasty   surgical operation to unblock a blood vessel

Looking inside

Sometimes people get pain in the **colon**. In the past they would have needed surgery. Now surgeons push a tube up through the **rectum**. This is called a **colonoscopy**.

The tube is called an **endoscope**. Surgeons use it to look inside the colon. A burning tool is used to get rid of problems, such as lumps.

This tool is being used inside the body. An electric current passes through a fine wire. It cuts off and seals harmful lumps.

colon   lower part of the large intestine

Stitches and scars could be a thing of the past. Wounds can now be closed with a zip! The special zip is called a Medizip (below). The Medizip is stuck onto the skin. Then it is simply zipped up.

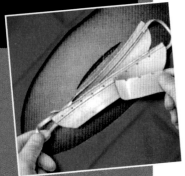

Latest news

New operations are being done all the time. Surgery is always in the news.

SURGEONS PLAN NEW LIVER TRANSPLANTS

There is a problem with **transplants**. To do them you need a healthy **organ**. But there are not enough to go round. Someone has to die before an organ can be used.

But British surgeons have made a breakthrough. They can use part of a living person's liver. **Donors** can give half of their own liver. This takes a few weeks to grow back.

A surgeon is sucking out fat from a woman's chin.

Surgical slimming

Now surgery can be used to make people thinner. Surgery is still risky though. A healthy diet and exercise are far safer ways to lose weight.

Some **obese** or very overweight people have their fat sucked out. This is called **liposuction**. The **surgeon** puts a tool under the skin. The tool sucks out the fatty liquid.

April 2004

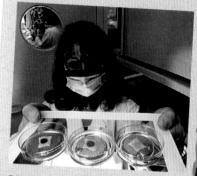

LIVING BANDAGES TO TREAT BURN VICTIMS

Very bad burns are hard to heal. But British scientists have found a new treatment. It uses living bandages called Myskin. They are made from the patient's skin **cells**.

Healthy skin cells are grown on small disks. These are planted on the wound. They help new skin to grow.

cell tiny unit that makes up all animal and plant tissue

New hand

In 1999 American **surgeons** did the first hand **transplant**. It took fifteen hours. The bones were joined with metal plates. The **blood vessels** and **nerves** were connected with stitches. Nerves are tissues that pass messages between the brain and the body.

And finally...

Sometimes surgery has to be done in an emergency. There may be no **antiseptics** to kill germs. There may be no **anesthetics** to stop the pain.

Self-surgery

In 2003 Aron Ralston was hiking in a **canyon** in Utah. He was alone. A boulder fell on Aron's arm. He could not get free. If he stayed there, he would die of thirst. Aron cut off his arm with a blunt penknife.

This is Aron Ralston. He is recovering from his self-surgery.

Word bank   **canyon** very deep and narrow valley

Surgery in the air

In 1995 Paula Dixon was on a plane. Suddenly she felt very ill. Dr. Angus Wallace and Dr. Tom Wong were on the plane, too. They rushed to the rescue.

Paula's lung had stopped working. The doctors dipped a coat hanger in brandy. This **sterilized** the wire. It made the wire clean. Then they poked the wire into her chest. They drained fluid out of her lung with a tube. Paula made a full recovery.

The future

There have been huge changes to surgery in the last 50 years. What changes will the next 50 years bring?

This surgeon has a **high-tech** device strapped to his head. It is part of a system that allows surgeons to see inside a patient's body.

sterilize   make clean by killing germs

Books

Bankston, John. *Joseph Lister and the Story of Antiseptics*. Hockessin, DE: Mitchell Lane, 2004.

Parker, Steve. *Groundbreakers: Alexander Fleming*. Chicago: Heinemann Library, 2001.

Solway, Andrew. *Hidden Life: What's Living Inside Your Body?* Chicago: Heinemann Library, 2004.

Using the Internet

The Internet can tell you more about medicine through the ages. You can use a search engine, such as www.yahooligans.com.

Type in keywords such as:

- Alexander Fleming
- history of medicine
- Louis Pasteur

Search tips

There are billions of pages on the Internet. It can be difficult to find what you are looking for.

These search tips will help you find useful websites more quickly:

- Know exactly what you want to find out about.
- Use two to six keywords in a search. Put the most important word first.
- Only use names of people, places or things.

Where to search

Search engine
A search engine looks through through millions of website ages. It lists all the sites that match the words in the search box. You will find the best matches are at the top of the list, on the first page.

Search directory
A person instead of a computer has sorted a search directory. You can search by keyword or subject and browse through the different sites. It is like looking through books on a library shelf.

Glossary

Aboriginal Australian native Australian

amputation removing part or all of a limb or other projecting body part

anesthetic drug to make patients sleep or to make treatment less painful

anatomy study of the structure of an animal or plant

angioplasty surgical operation to unblock a blood vessel

antibiotic medicine that kills harmful bacteria

antiseptic chemical that stops harmful bacteria from growing and spreading disease

appendix organ attached to the large intestine. It has no use in the human body.

bacteria group of tiny living things that can cause diseases

barber surgeon barber who also did minor surgery, mainly for the poor

bloodletting cutting the skin or a vein to let blood flow out

blood vessel narrow tube inside the body that carries blood

calcium crystals material that also makes up bones and teeth

canyon very deep and narrow valley

carbolic acid chemical that can kill bacteria

catgut strong thread made from the intestines of sheep. It is used in surgery.

cauterize burn a wound with a hot instrument

cell tiny unit that makes up all animal and plant tissue

chloroform colorless liquid with a strong smell, used as an anesthetic

civil war when soldiers from the same country fight each other

colon lower part of the large intestine

colonoscopy looking inside the colon with an endoscope

donor person whose body parts or blood are used in transplant operations

endoscope instrument for seeing inside the body

ether chemical first used as an anesthetic in the 1800s

field hospital temporary hospital, often in a tent near the battlefield

firebomb bomb designed to start a fire

gall bladder organ that stores bile. This helps in digestion.

gangrene when flesh rots and dies due to lack of blood supply. Infection can do this.

gladiator person trained to fight with weapons

graft piece of living skin that is planted on another part of the body with surgery

high-tech using the most up-to-date technology

infected when tiny living things grow in the body and cause diseases

lanced surgically cut into

laser very strong beam of light that is used in surgery for burning or cutting

liposuction sucking out fat from under the skin

medical about the treatment of diseases and injuries

Middle Ages period in European history between AD 500 and 1500

nerve bundle of fibers that take electrical signals from parts of the body to the brain and back again

nitrous oxide colorless gas used as an anesthetic

obese very overweight

opium drug made from opium poppies. It helps people to relax and to relieve pain.

organ part of the body that does a certain job

pressure force that builds up in a space and cannot escape

pus thick green or yellow liquid made by infected wounds. It often smells bad.

reconstructive putting something back together again

rectum end part of the large intestine. It is joined to the anus.

scalp skin on top of the head where the hair grows

scalpel knife with a small, sharp blade

shrapnel tiny pieces of metal thrown out in an explosion

sterilize make clean by killing germs

surgeon doctor who operates on the body

survive stay alive

transplant when a part of a body is taken out of one person and put into another person

trench large ditch dug to shelter from enemy attack

trepanning drilling a hole through the skull

tumor growth or swelling in the body that is not normal

turpentine oil and resin mixture that comes from pine trees

ultrasound very high sound waves that we cannot hear

Index